LEGO STAR WARS™

SECRETS
OF THE
DARK SIDE

Written by Matt Jones

Editor Matt Jones
Senior Designer Lauren Adams
Designers Sunita Gahir, Elena Jarmoskaite
Pre-production Producer Kavita Varma
Producer Louise Daly
Managing Editor Paula Regan
Design Manager Jo Connor
Publisher Julie Ferris
Art Director Lisa Lanzarini
Publishing Director Simon Beecroft

First published in Great Britain in 2017
by Dorling Kindersley Limited
80 Strand, London, WC2R 0RL

Page design copyright © 2017 Dorling Kindersley Limited
A Penguin Random House Company

17 18 19 20 10 9 8 7 6 5 4 3 2 1

001–299071–10/17

A CIP catalogue record for this book
is available from the British Library.

ISBN: 978-0-2412-8536-7

Printed and bound in China

A WORLD OF IDEAS:
SEE ALL THERE IS TO KNOW

www.LEGO.com/starwars
www.starwars.com
www.dk.com

Contents

The Force

The Force is a great power.
It has a light side and a
dark side.
The light side is used for good.

Darth Vader

The dark side is used for evil.
Luke Skywalker is a Jedi.
He uses the light side.
Darth Vader is a Sith.
He uses the dark side.

Luke Skywalker

Darth Sidious

Darth Sidious leads the Sith.
He does not like the Jedi.
He wants to control the galaxy!

6

Stormtrooper   Stormtrooper Sergeant

Snowtrooper   Sandtrooper

Armoured troops

The Sith have many troops.
They wear different armour.
They can fight in the snow,
sand and water.

Shoretrooper   Scout Trooper

Darth Maul

Darth Maul is a scary Sith!
He is from the planet Dathomir.

Maul has horns on his head.
He has a special lightsaber
with two red blades.

Count Dooku

Count Dooku was once a Jedi.
Now he has joined the Sith.

The Jedi want to find him.
He escapes from the Jedi
on his speeder bike.

Anakin Skywalker

Asajj Ventress

Asajj Ventress is a strong Sith.
She uses two red lightsabers.
She tries to defeat Anakin
Skywalker in battle.

Asajj Ventress

TIE Interceptor

Speedy vehicles

The Sith and their troops
have lots of vehicles.
They can battle in space,
the air or on the ground.

Star Destroyer

AT-AT

Darth Vader

The powerful Darth Vader
was once hurt in battle.
Now he has to wear a suit
of armour to protect his body.

Kylo Ren

Kylo Ren uses the dark side of the Force.

Kylo wants to rule the galaxy.

Kylo Ren

Rey uses the light side
of the Force.
Can Rey stop Kylo Ren?

Rey

Quiz

1. Who leads the Sith?

2. Why does Darth Vader wear a suit of armour?

3. Which Sith uses two lightsabers?

4. Who has horns on his head?

5. Who escapes from the Jedi on a speeder bike?

Answers on page 23

Index

Answers to the quiz on page 22
1. Darth Sidious
2. To protect his body
3. Asajj Ventress
4. Darth Maul
5. Count Dooku

A Note to Parents

THIS BOOK is part of an exciting four-level reading series for children, developing the habit of reading widely for both pleasure and information.

Beautiful illustrations and superb full-colour images combine with engaging, easy-to-read narratives to offer a fresh approach to each subject in the series. Each book is guaranteed to capture a child's interest while developing his or her reading skills, general knowledge and love of reading.

The four levels of reading books are aimed at different reading abilities, enabling you to choose the books that are exactly right for your child:

Level 1: Learning to read
Level 2: Beginning to read
Level 3: Beginning to read alone
Level 4: Reading alone

The "normal" age at which a child begins to read can be anywhere from three to eight years old. Adult participation through the lower levels is very helpful for providing encouragement, discussing storylines and sounding out unfamiliar words.

No matter which level you select, you can be sure that you are helping your child learn to read, then read to learn!